CW00956892

The Tao of
My Thoughts

The Tao of
My Thoughts

By.

[signature]

Seahorse Books
Offchurch, Warwickshire

Seahorse Books

1 Bunkers' Hill Cottages,
Welsh Road,
Offchurch,
Leamington Spa,
Warwickshire.
CV33 9BE
www.SeahorseArts.co.uk

First published 2006

Published by Seahorse Books.

©Seahorse Books 2006

Chee Soo asserts the moral right to
be identified as the author of this work.

ISBN 0954524454
Printed and bound in Great Britain by
Creative Print and Design, (Ebbw Vale) Wales.

Wood free - this book is printed on purely recycled paper.

Editor's note

A strange thing happened today, something quite unexpected.

I just happened to be visiting an old friend when quite out of the blue a new manuscript came to light. Well in actual fact it was an old manuscript.

Inside was a diary written over many years as far back as the 1970's with Chee's thoughts about Taoist philosophy, over a hundred pages with hand drawn pictures in Chinese inks, quite remarkable. As I leafed through it I must confess a tear came to my eye. I was lost for words.

She said she was entrusting this book to me in case anything happened to her and said I could do as I wished with it. So on the way home I stuffed it into an old jiffy bag to keep it safe, and the funny thing is when I got home my attention was drawn to the label on the bag. It was from the printers of Chee's books, somehow it had got into the back seat of my car I don't know how, very strange.

Well anyway, considering this I thought it would be selfish really to keep all this to myself now wouldn't it?

So here's the result.

Chris Simpson

Taoist Cultural Arts Association

Monday 20th February 2006

Contents

Acknowledgements

We would like to give our sincerest thanks and gratitude to Marilyn and Chee Soo for all the support they have given us over the years and without whom this book would not have been possible.

Thanks also to Rachel and Asher Simpson for all the help they gave in the preparation of this book.

Chris Simpson (Editor)

FOREWORD

These thoughts started to come to me on the 20th December 1976, and after two hours they were still entering my brain, so it occurred to me that others, like yourself, might like to share them with me, and perhaps even try to live by their principles. So for the last eight years I have jotted them down, whenever time permitted.

Always remember, that Taoism is not a religion, for it encompasses all beliefs and religions, for it came into being more than 10,000 years B.C. It is a way of living in accordance with the natural laws of nature, and in complete harmony with the energies of the universe, and following the ordained WAY of life as laid down by the TAO.

It is therefore, a very deep ingrained philosophy and harmonises naturally with everything around us, and within us.

So, after reading through these thoughts that came to me, if you feel deep down inside that they have influenced your life, either through your mental, physical or spiritual spheres, then the WAY (Tao) is now wide open for you to understand, to live with, and assist others every day of your life.

May the TAO always be with you on your journey through your life.

Chee Soo.

INTRODUCTION

The Tao, is the ordained Way, it is the absolute truth, and it is the life of everything within the entire universe and beyond. Whilst all three are ONE in principle, each has its own field of work, its own sphere of influence, and its own meaning within our lives, and within nature. It is certainly not the mystical complex that so many Western people believe, or make it out to be.

The simple truth is, that those who believe or say that Taoism is just an out-dated mystical religion, are not Taoists themselves, so how can they sit back and make such remarks when they haven't got the foggiest idea what it is all about. Not only are these people sceptics, but worse than that, they are also blind to the world around them, but also, they cannot even see themselves, and therefore they should be pitied, and they certainly have our deepest sympathy for their dire handicap.

Because human beings have got into the habit of thinking about the most trivial things, and formulating their own ideas about this and that, constantly making plans about what they are going to do next, and for tomorrow, and the day after, even next week or next month. They automatically dissect everything and anything, and just by starting off with one thought, within seconds it has multiplied ten-fold, in fact, the thoughts become so uncontrollable that they flit in and out of the brain, just like a host of flies.

If they were told that it is absolutely a complete waste of time and energy to go to such lengths, and that they would save many years of unnecessary trouble and constant experimentation. If they simply stopped trying to do everything and anything, and just learn to accept life as it comes, instead of pushing all the time, they would think you were mad.

How could they accept that everything in the universe is following its own pre-destined and ordained way of life, and because this is the simple yet absolute truth, there are many who, because of their multitude of thoughts see something mysterious, or think there is something mysterious, even in the most natural growth of things. So anyone who lives by the natural order of life, like the Taoist, is automatically branded a weirdy, a freak, or even a mystic.

Maybe, because the Taoist is fully aware of the true meaning of the very simple rules that have been laid down by the Supreme Spirit (Yuhuang Tati), and they are extremely simple, they perhaps do not make the same dynamic impression or impact on the human mind, that perhaps, a more seemingly complex problem could make. So, perhaps, that is one of the reasons why so many people in the West find it hard to understand. Because it is so simple and so very easy, and because it goes far deeper than their normal every day comprehension, they immediately think that it is abnormal, and therefore, perhaps, even a little bit mysterious.

What they have to understand is that everything within the universe follows its own unalterable course, and that course or WAY was planned for it long before it came into life. Most people do not give this part of their lives a second thought, and they do, in fact, take it all for granted. The curious part about it all, is, that everyone accepts it, and many things like it, every day of their lives, without trying to understand it. Do you realise that your own personal sex was ordained to be before your parents had intercourse, in fact, it was decided long before they had even met. (If the Tao wills it, one day we will have the opportunity of proving this simple fact to you).

After all, as we have said before, night follows day, day follows night, each season automatically follows one another, and the cycle of the year commences when the old one has been completed. Who do you think planned it all? Yes! this is all accepted without thought or without question, and therefore it is all taken for granted quite naturally.

So it happens, as well, in all the other fields of nature, the trees and the flowers send out their new shoots every spring, and they bloom during specific periods in the summer months, and then they fade away and die in the autumn and the winter, to rest, until the cycle starts again the next year. Vapour forms the clouds in the sky, clouds in turn create the rain, rain nurtures the soil, enabling the ground to become more fertile. These are also the natural cycle of events that take place in life continuously, yet humanity does not query these changes, or ask the reason why - they accept it. Simply because it doesn't matter, and you don't even have to ask, for it is completely natural.

However, by your acceptance of all these things, that are completely natural - then you have shown to yourself and to the world, that you have automatically accepted and recognised the TAO, and this is the first step in your own appreciation, understanding, and awareness. You have, by your own automatic action, and, without even giving it another thought, received the TAO into your own daily life - and that life, has adjusted itself to the natural manifestations of the universe, which, in turn, is abiding by its own immutable progress through the realms of time and space.

THE SUPREME AND ABSOLUTE

In the very beginning of time, and long before time began, and long before there was even a universe. In fact, long before there was nothing, there was the non-existence of nothing, and, before that, there was the void, and it was, and still is, the home of the Supreme and Absolute Force (Tsuikao Wanch'uan) or more commonly known as the Supreme Spirit (Yuang Tati), that controls everything within and without, the whole universe.

The Supreme and Absolute Power or Force, is not a he or a she, for it is a dynamic ball or field of energy, which is so powerful that it is beyond the imaginations of a normal human being.

During one period, the Supreme Force noticed that all its energy was just a seething mass, it was swirling here and there, rotating in circles, moving forward and back, left and right, completely out of control, and was burning itself out needlessly, by its constant movement and fluctuation, and it was all sheer chaos and utter confusion. So The Supreme Spirit decided to organise everything, by starting with the animating principles of its own energy.

This is how the TAO came into being, for the TAO is the laid down orders, principles, rules, codes, the way that everything in the entire cosmos must diligently follow, it is the road or path that all things have to adhere to rigidly throughout their entire existence. To put it in simple words, the TAO is the unwritten law and instructions that govern every single thing, from its commencement or birth, through its complete span of life or activity, to its death, extinction or complete wane. The TAO is the laws or principles laid down by the Supreme Force or Spirit, to cover and apply to each and everything, that was, that is, and what will be. It is the divine WILL of the Supreme and Absolute Force or Spirit.

In the very beginning The Supreme Force or Spirit created order from the chaos that existed, and it ordained that everything should have a balance of two influences, just like a house with a front and a back, a box with a top and a bottom, or our bodies with a left side and a right side, and this duality, which forms an integral part of everything in the universe, the ancient Taoists of China described them as the Yin and Yang. So from the one TAO came the orders of the two principles which determine the stability of all creation, and also control all the processes of evolution and changes that take place within it. So it was the energy, which we call macro-cosmic energy (Ching Sheng Li), of the Supreme Force or Spirit, that was the first to be directed by the TAO, and the first to be affected by this simple duality.

It was from this duality of the Supreme Force or Spirit, that the universe was created more than five billion years ago, and by the way, dinosaurs roamed the earth about twenty four million years ago, whereas human beings are only about five million years old, so there is quite a big difference in time levels.

Because everything had to conform to this duality, then even the Yin and Yang had to have two sides, plus a neutral zone between the two, which gave them a total of five sections, which the Taoists named as the "Five Elements" (Wu Hsing), and it was from these simple yet positive foundations that all life, and everything within nature became possible.

It all started off, after the creation of this earth, with the life of the vegetation, then came the fishes, and then the mammals, then finally the human race, and that is how we came into existence, through the will of the TAO, and how we have been here ever since.

Though the TAO and its Yin and Yang constituents fill Heaven and Earth, they cannot be seen by the normal eye-sight, yet they are visible to the mind, soul, and to the spirit. They are insubstantial yet they are a composite substance of the material and the immaterial; they naturally yield to change but are themselves positively absolute; their power is beyond normal human comprehension and yet their gentleness is softer than the air that touches the face. They are internal as well as external, they are micro-cosmic as well as macro-cosmic, they can also be both passive and active simultaneously whilst linking through their contermination. They are completely individual, yet, at the same time they are an harmonious part of each other - this, has therefore created the Dual Monism, which is the combined unity and diversity of the entire cosmos.

Unless the human race learns to accept the TAO, and live by the basic rules of the Yin and Yang, and the Five Elements, and learns to follow the unwritten yet natural laws of the Supreme Force or Spirit, then the human race will wither away and die.

Chapter 1.

The Tao

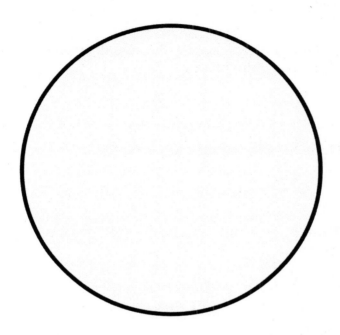

The Void, a seething mass of dynamic energy is the home of the TAO, and it is also the centre of the entire cosmos, and it is due to this energy, under the strict rules and control of the TAO, that everything is ordained to be, everything has its rightful place in the universe and in our world. Whatever happens, even the slightest (what we would call) accident was meant to be, for everything consists of the Yin and Yang, which are the integral parts of the TAO.

1. There is only one beginning, but many endings, let us pray for the time when both are joined together, and the beginning has finished, and the ending has begun, then our life will be in constant harmony with the TAO.

2. If there is peace amidst the tumult, then the TAO has found its rightful place.

3. Never tell a lie, for the truth is the TAO.

4. There is never stillness, for the TAO is constantly on the move.

5. The TAO is the highway to Heaven, so learn to memorise the route.

6. There is no such thing as good luck or misfortune, for they are the natural movements of the TAO.

7. We are one with the TAO, who made us, then let us try to retain this unity, throughout our lives.

8.   The TAO ensures that everything has its just reward.

9.   Non-action does not mean that you sit back and simply do nothing - it is just the acceptance of the natural world around you, which, of course, is the TAO.

10.   The TAO is always visible, you have only to open your eyes and you will see it.

11.   Efficiency lies where there is nothing - and a wheel is a very good example of this - so always remember, that the TAO is the centre of everything, and therefore it is the hub of the Void.

12.   It is only when you begin to see the TAO in the streets, that you can honestly say that your eyes are beginning to open.

13.   Yes! The TAO is your eyes, your mind, and your spirit, so all you have to do is to harmonise all of them - and when you have done so, then eventually the "WAY" will be made known to you personally.

14.   Men and women look in different ways, for they both have to conform to the laws of the TAO.

15. When you are protected by the TAO, no harm will ever come to you.

16. If life means nothing to you, then turn to the TAO for guidance and wisdom.

17. Motion can be very fast, but motionless can be even faster, and the TAO is both.

18. There is no such thing as an accident, it is simply a pre-arranged event created by the TAO.

19. The wise try to understand the TAO, the ignorant try to understand evil.

20. The person of the TAO is a constant servant, for he or she serves the TAO on the one hand, and people on the other.

21. If you have the TAO with you constantly, then you are the richest person in the world.

22. Everything is difficult unless you conform to the wishes of the TAO.

23. Don't focus on a light, it is materialistic; focus on the TAO, and everything will be made known to you.

24. Switch on the light of the TAO within yourself, and give illumination to the world.

25. The TAO made everything complete, don't try and break it into pieces.

26. The TAO will show you the pathway to Heaven, if you can see it properly.

27. The soul is within and the spirit is without, so this dualism creates perfect harmony into one - and that one is the TAO.

28. The TAO is invisible, yet it can always be seen - so train yourself to see it.

29. Doing nothing means doing everything BUT in accordance with the laws of the TAO.

30. We are children of the universe, so why not let the TAO help us to mature.

31. If you can see the TAO, then you will never lose your way in life.

32. Don't look for the road, for the TAO is already there in front of you.

33. A sage is not a person, it is just another expression of the TAO.

34. We live in a world that is constantly changing, so why not learn to accept it - and you will learn that it is just another sign that the TAO is showing you that it is on the move.

35. If you do not listen to the TAO, then you will certainly create trouble for yourself.

36. First, learn to see; secondly, learn to be conscious; and thirdly, learn to understand; these are the initial basic steps you should take to appreciate the TAO.

37. Heaven is not something that is beyond our reach, for the TAO is all around you now as you are reading this - just join us in recognising it.

38. Words are the expression of the body, understanding is the impression on the mind, and living is the conception of the spirit - and the TAO is the governor of all three.

39. Emptiness is the birthplace of the TAO.

40. Breath is the essence of life, and life is the essence of the spirit, whilst the spirit is the essence of the TAO. Harmonise all three and your spiritual growth is assured.

41. The earth is the foundation of a house, the universe is the foundation of our earth, but the TAO is the constant foundation of them all.

In harmony with the TAO because of the Yin and Yang aspect.

42.   Speech can be incoherent, meaningless, distorted and
       empty, and therefore can mean absolutely nothing.
       Silence, on the other hand, can tell a complete story and
       create a million deeds, and therefore it can mean
       everything in our life. So hunt diligently, and one day
       you may find the Silence that you are looking for - and
       when you do, you will have truly found the TAO.

43. Nothing is too large or too small that it cannot be encompassed by the TAO.

44. There is no easy way out from a difficult situation unless the TAO opens the door for you.

45. What is intangible is tangible. What is immaterial is materialistic. What is insubstantial is substantial and even if you reversed each one, then they would still be the same. This is the TAO.

46. If you enjoy music, then you are listening to the TAO.

47. If you walk with the TAO, then you will always have light within your darkness.

48. You were born according to the will of the TAO, then learn to abide by its rules.

49. To the ignorant life is a constant mystery, but to the man or woman of the TAO, then life is a clear open road.

50.   The TAO is the dual monism of the universe.

51.   The TAO is like your shadow, always with you and always connected to you, but is separated from you.

52.   Separation and unification are the transformations of Kuan Yin, who is also a part of the TAO.

53.   Christians celebrate the birth of Jesus Christ once a year. The Taoist celebrates it every day of his life.

54.   The TAO is the centre of the universe, for all directions emanate from it.

55.   The TAO is the father of the five elements, which, in turn is the father of all energies, and which, in turn, is the father of all phenomena within the universe.

56.   Achievement is a natural fulfilment of the TAO, so words are unnecessary.

57. The TAO creates harmony and peace, and it is only humans that create violence.

58. No church or temple need ever to be built, for the temple of the TAO is the universe.

59. Many appreciate the light of the day, but cannot understand the darkness of the night, yet both are part of the TAO.

60. The room of your life has many doors, but only one leads to the TAO, make sure you choose the right one.

61. Never be afraid, for the TAO is always with you.

62. The TAO made the world, and it is with us every day of our lives, but very few recognise it in the street.

63. The ignorant look at yesterday, the intelligent look at tomorrow, the wise look at today - but the Taoist Sage only looks at this minute.

64.   The TAO is the highway of your life, so be prepared to meet all types of people along it.

65.   If you have a "lucky break", a "winning streak", or a spate of "good luck", then thank the TAO who had arranged it for you.

66.   When reason has disappeared, sanity must take its place. When sanity disappears then the TAO must replace it, or otherwise chaos will reign.

67.   You cannot wrap a fire in paper, but you can wrap the flames of your life with the TAO, and thereby gain constant protection.

68.   If your load is too heavy to bear, then hand it over to the TAO, who will be happy to carry it for you.

69.   The TAO is as old as eternity, but as young as this very second. So it has all the vitality of youth, plus all the experience of a billion years.

70. Don't be trapped at the bottom of a well, enjoy the freedom of the TAO.

71. If you work in harmony with the TAO, then you no longer have to worry or deliberate.

72. Only awareness will give you the complete understanding of the TAO.

73. If you do not plan, then everything will work out exactly as it was ordained to be, for the TAO will look after your interests constantly.

74. Everything that happens in your life, is an experience, so thank the TAO for the knowledge it is giving to you.

75. Those who understand the TAO become a part of it.

76. Physical exercise is the expression of man, mental activity is the expression of the energies, motionless and stillness is the expression of the TAO.

77.   If you are a part of the TAO, then you can bear the unbearable.

78.   If you truly follow the TAO, then you will automatically follow your true destiny.

79.   If you try to push the TAO, then not only will you burn up your energies, and thereby create greater stress, but you will also fail to reach your objective.

80.   Awareness of the TAO creates great satisfaction, but don't fall into the human trap of worrying about it so much that you lose it.

81.   Whilst there is the Void, there will be immaculate control.

82.   If you accept the change of the day and of the night, then you have already taken the first step in your recognition of the TAO.

83.   To the Taoist the unexpected is not strange, it is just a sign of the TAO.

84. Those who understand the TAO appreciate its principles. Those who understand the principles appreciate the changes. Those who understand the changes will appreciate the complete fullness of life. Those who understand the fullness of life will live for ever.

85. Before the universe there was the void. Before the void there was non-entity. Before non-entity there was non-existence. Before non-existence there was nothing. Before nothing there was (something or other, but I can't find a word for it). So even though there is a   there is always something. For that is the TAO.

86. There is no such thing as emptiness, nor is there a void. Everything has fullness, and such fullness has movement. And all movement is under the control of the Yin and Yang.
     These, in turn, take their instruction from the TAO.

     A cup can be turned upside down, yet it still remains full.
     A hole can be dug in the ground, yet it is not emptied.
     A gale can subside, but there is still the motion behind.
     Whenever there is a VOID there is usefulness.
     A bowl is not a bowl without the emptiness in the middle.
     A wheel cannot be a wheel without the hole for the hub.
     No one can talk without the gap between the lips.

     There would be no whirlpool without the nothing in the centre.
     A whirlwind would go berserk if it did not obtain its rotary guidance through the central space.
     There would be no universe without the strict adherence to the laws of the VOID.

This is the TAO, which is, the absolute control of the centre of the VOID.

The VOID, in itself, is the essential usefulness around which everything in outer space is held together.

The outer space is the universe of which we are only a very small fragment.

Learn to accept it every minute of every day, and conform to the natural laws that govern our lives.

Chapter 2

Yin and Yang

The Yin and Yang are the negative and positive sides of everything within the universe, and were formulated by the Taoists of ancient China, some five thousand years ago. They were first seen in a materialistic way carved on the Stone Drums about one thousand years B.C.

Eventually, Yang came to represent Heaven, Light, Male, Tall, Long, Penetration, Oddness in numbers, The Monad, Mountains, and it is symbolized by the Dragon.

Yin however, is used to represent the Earth world, Darkness, Females, Smallness, Short, Absorption, Even numbers, The Duad, the Valleys and Streams, and it is symbolized by the Tiger.

1.   Even the TAO has its Yin and Yang.

2.   What keeps the Yin and Yang apart, yet harmonises them
      both so that they are kept together?   It is the TAO, the
      centre and extreme of all things.

3.   When two are together and combine as one, then they
      will have their ups and downs - but when two are One
      yet each remain separate, then there will be constant
      harmony. This is the Yin and Yang, which is Dual
      Monism, which is the TAO.

4.   Thunder when there is a clear blue sky, is just another
      aspect of the Yin and Yang - but it also lets you know that
      the TAO can create the impossible.

5.   Yin and Yang are not separate parts of the universe, for
      one cannot exist without the other -   for the TAO
      harmonises both of them.

6.   We live in a Yin world, so be happy, for the Yang is yet to
      come.

7.   Everything in life is a balance of the Yin and Yang, why not learn to recognise them in your daily life?

8.   The Yin contracts, the Yang expands, so both go in opposite directions. Yet when harmonised, they become one, in both directions at the same time.

9.   Man (Yang) is born of woman (Yin), so man should be eternally grateful by trying to keep this harmony all through his life.

10.   Only when you have suffered can you fully appreciate what true happiness really means - this is the Yin and Yang of our emotions.

11.   Through gentleness one is strong.
      Through suppleness one is active.
      Through yielding one is unmoveable.
      Through unity one is inseparable.
      This is the Yin and Yang of our emotions.

12.   The home of the spirit is Heaven which is Yang.
      The home of humans is the Earth which is Yin.
      This is the duality within our own personal lives.

13. Everything is born of Yin, so extreme Yin will always overcome extreme Yang.

14. Yin and Yang are dualism and monism, for they can remain separate entities, and yet they can harmonise and become one - the TAO.

15. Joy and sorrow are the extremes of the Yin and Yang and are expressions of our emotions - but non-indulgence in either, will always ensure equilibrium, for the TAO is always the balance.

16. If you make a mistake, look around you for the TAO, for that was a Yin occurrence, and the Yang will automatically follow.

17. In the summer of 1976, constant sunshine created a drought, and the politicians constantly talked about spending millions of pounds (Stirling) on reservoirs and water pipes. If they had had a true understanding of the TAO, then they would have realized that the Yin always follows the Yang, and it was only a matter of waiting.

18. A poor start will mean a good finish - this is the Yin and Yang of a journey.

19. I was born an orphan, with no known father or mother and with no known relations - yet today, in my old age, I have a family of millions living and practising our Taoist Arts. This is, therefore, the Yin and Yang of my own family life.

20. What is possible is made by the will of the TAO. What is impossible is acceptance of the will of the TAO. This is the Yin and Yang aspects of possibilities which are created by the TAO.

21. Humanity survives from the goodness of the earth, but their destiny is reliant on the TAO - this is the Yin and Yang of human existence.

22. Those who abide by the will of the TAO are always healthy. Those who oppose the will of the TAO are always sick. This is the Yin and Yang of good health.

23. Spring and Summer are Yang whereas Autumn and Winter are Yin - so they encompass the Yin and Yang seasons of the year.

24. Yin creates life, Yang destroys it - how many parents suffer the agony of their own actions?

25.   From the formlessness of the VOID, order came first, then the Yin and the Yang, and then the universe was created.

26.   We gather from the Earth to store, and we store to spread it all over the Earth, and thereby the farmer conforms to the Yin and Yang.

27.   When there is no beginning, there can be no end - which is a simple law of Yin and Yang.

28.   By being materialistic man misses out on the immaterial, and therefore his Yang has no Yin, and he is out of balance with his life.

29.   Those who freeze in the winter look forward to the heat of the summer - and those who have a Yin life on earth can look forward to the Yang life to come.

30.   The greatest ship can sink, the finest house can fall, the richest man can lose. All this is opportunity - the opportunity to advance and the opportunity to retire. This becomes timing - the timing of the Yin and Yang, in accordance with the laws of the TAO.

31. When the journey comes to an end, then the beginning
     commences.

32. What is possible is made by the will of the TAO. What is
     impossible is the acceptance of the will of the TAO. This
     is the Yin and Yang aspects of possibilities which are
     created by the TAO.

33. Life begins with joy, but it always ends with sadness - for
     this is the Yin and Yang of our emotions.

34. Every symptom must have a cause - for this is the Yin and
     Yang of sickness.

35. What others start, we must learn to complete - this is the
     Yin and Yang of work.

36. If you can make a word, then you can create a sentence.

37. If you hear thunder when there is a blue sky, then watch
     out for the rain and the black sky, for this is the Yin and
     Yang of the weather.

38.   As the windmill rotates, and the watermill turns, and the wheels spin, and as day turns into night, and spring follows winter, the TAO changes into its Yin and Yang components every minute of every day of your life - be aware of it, watch its progress, understand its fluctuations, and you will become an integral part of the universe.

39.   When a person lives in the luxury of a penthouse, eating the finest of food, and drinking the finest wines, his head is automatically in the clouds. So he must be forgiven for not keeping his feet on the ground and his spirit in Heaven, for he has lost touch with the Yin and Yang essences of his own life.

40.   For two million years man has led every sphere of life on this Earth, and now the next two million years will be the turn of the women. In other words, the Yang phase of human life has nearly completed its circle, and very slowly it will soon be the turn of the Yin. So after maximum expansion has been reached, then contraction will automatically take place. This is the will of the TAO.

41.   Have you noticed that girls and women (Yin) are getting most of the top marks in schools and colleges, and getting a lot of the top jobs in industry. Whereas more and more men are having to stay at home, looking after the children and cooking the meals. It will soon be very common place.

Chapter 3

Nature

The whole of nature is an integral part of the universe, whether it is known or unknown, all animals, humans, and everything that was and is being born in the sea, and all vegetation, whether it is large, gigantic, small or minute, was, and is, completely natural phenomena which have been created by the Supreme Energy, on the explicit instructions of the TAO.

1. Although water can fly in the clouds, it cannot go uphill.

2. Although snow is white on top, it is black underneath.

3. Water always starts at the top and flows down to the lowest level, pity man does not emulate nature.

4. Every physical illness is man made, but only nature can cure it.

5. Before you reach the top of the tree, you have to traverse many branches.

6. If you want the world to perish, then spoil the waters.

7. Everything in nature is in perfect balance, it is man that tips the scales.

8. The Lotus is to the Chinese, what Man should be to nature.

9. The trees stand bare and the snow lies on the ground, and in the distance the birds are singing. Within all nature there is peace.

10. Water is a part of everything for even our body comprises 90% fluid, so why is man trying to kill himself by polluting the waters?

11. Salmon swims upstream against the flow of water, yet it does so in accordance with the laws of nature. Man unfortunately, does this all the time, but in opposition to the laws of nature.

12. We are as much a part of nature as the trees and the birds, then let us accept our environment and our growth.

13. The reflection on a pool of water, never shows its depth.

14. Everything in nature is perfect, let us try and be the same.

15. Fish will die out of water, so learn to live in your own environment.

16. Those who accept a rose, must also learn that they are also accepting the thorns.

17. Notice how the trees bend and give way before the strong winds. Man should learn to emulate nature.

18. Man is like a fish out of water - he has left his natural environment.

19. The TAO gave the earth the ability to grow good wholesome food, so why does man try to change both with chemicals?

20. Certainly admire the fruit and blooms on the trees and bushes, but don't forget the roots which gave them their beauty, and don't forget the TAO that created everything,

21. Everything within nature has a tendency to bind together, why is it that man cannot do the same?

22. Have you ever tried to catch the dust in a wind? Trust nature to be one step ahead of you.

23. Everything in nature has something in common - then why don't we emulate nature?

24. If you can enjoy the fruits of nature, then why not enjoy the fruits that other people can offer?

25. Just because there are a few rotten fruits on the tree, you don't chop it down, do you? Then why do people have to die, through the use of drugs, because they have an odd symptom?

26. We all accept that birds have different colours, then why can't we accept this same principle amongst humans?

27. If you beat the grass to frighten the snakes - then watch out for the rebound, for you are trying to use nature against nature and there are bound to be repercussions.

28. If you cannot live out on the grass and under the sky, then watch out - for you are losing your touch with nature - and the end cannot be far away.

29. True life is a boomerang, for it always returns.

30.   Water may be held in the highest point in the clouds, yet it can, in turn, become a part of the sewers. So always remember, that no one can attain such a height that he cannot become a part of the lowest.

31.   When the sun sets, it is not the end of the day; and this also applies to our own life.

32.   Be like the lotus, rise up from the mud, and from the depths of the pool of your life, and show yourself to the world.

33.   We all share everything of nature, then why not let nature share everything of ours?

34.   When the crane disappears from this earth, then the whole world will become desolate.

35.   The valley cannot reach the top of the mountain, but the top of the mountain can easily join the valley.

36.   Flowers express the beauty of nature; nature expresses the beauty of the TAO, so we must, therefore, just like the flowers, learn to express the true beauty of ourselves.

37. The leaves are turning colour and beginning to fall, but it is only one of the many expressions of the Yin period which is created by the TAO.

38. The snow outside blankets the whole countryside, like the TAO which covers everything.

39. The TAO has planted the trees, so that everything and everyone can enjoy the fruits and the shade.

40. The gale turns the boats over and smashes them on to the shore, and yet the seagull rides the wind just as if it was only a gentle breeze. The person of the TAO is a seagull every day of his life.

41. Without air the body will die, without food the body will perish; then thank the TAO for having created nature so that we can all live.

42. Everything in nature was born for a purpose. Then why not try and find out what the TAO expects of you?

43. Nature shows its beauty in the countryside, but finds it difficult to do so in the city, which was made by man who loves to live in ugliness.
Learn to follow the TAO and you will find beauty everywhere, in the town as well as the countryside.

44. The whole of nature has its active periods and its rest periods - but even in its rest periods it does not stop, because everything within the TAO is in constant motion.

45. No stream can run smoothly all the time, for there are always ripples caused by stones, rocks, waterfalls, and even the wind - and our life is exactly the same, but we must learn to accept it as it comes, just like the water does - for it is all a part of nature. It is part of the TAO.

46. A dog is a very wise animal, for in the wild he would have to fend for himself, but as a pet of humans he gets his food and comfort completely free all the time - and even man cannot match that.

47. A mouse can frighten an elephant, and an ant can scare a mouse. It is the tiniest that has the greatest power.

48. Those who treasure wealth, cannot truly appreciate the real treasures of nature, which is around them.

49. Your ancestors nurtured the roots, so now you can truly enjoy the flowers and the fruits of the tree. Well! just do the same for the next generation.

50. You may dip your oar in the river a million times, but you won't catch the same water.

51. A stick grows in peace as an integral part of nature, so why does man cut it down, trim it, and turn it into a weapon of war?

52. Herbal therapy has been proved for thousands of years, modern chemical medicines should also be proved over the same period, before they are issued to the general public.

53. Because water and fire do not mix, they are both used against one another - for completely opposite functions.

54. When you see the height of the waves, then you will appreciate the strength of the wind.

55. If you have to nestle in the long grass, then you have one consolation, nature is protecting you.

56. In China, Soya beans and Seaweed are used extensively to cure nutritional anaemia. Nature can always come to the aid of all animal life.

57. Without the wonders of nature, all humanity would die.

58. When you call a Blackbird black, are you being a racist?

Chapter 4

Humanity

The beginnings of the Human Race started over twenty million years ago, but in all this time they still haven't learnt to live and work together - for the benefits of all humans everywhere.

1.   Those who do not participate, will not be involved.

2.   If you are going on a long journey, make sure that you are fully prepared.

3.   The more the rules say DO NOT, the more the actions of man say DO.

4.   Those who help the birth of violence, have no option but to watch its growth.

5.   The greater the love, the more extreme the hate.

6.   When two become truly harmonised, they become as one.

7.   Everyone moves at their own speed in life, so therefore learn to give way to the fast, and do not despise the slow.

8.   If you do not have, therefore you can never lose.

37.   Accept life as it is, and don't try to solve tomorrow's problems, for the TAO has the answers already.

38.   If you are emotional, then you have lost control of yourself, and you are, therefore, out of touch with the TAO.

39.   There are many humans who will search and search, yet they never find. If they would only understand properly and hold hands with the TAO, then they would not have to search any more.

40.   We were born with nothing, and we will die with nothing, so why can't we be happy with nothing?

41.   If you will always put things into grades and standards, then you will always have the rich and poor, and the good and bad.

42.   When you are physically tired, mentally exhausted, and your spirit is weary, then it is about time you called on the TAO for help.

43. Even though your body grows older, you are as young as
     your spiritual growth.

44. All humanity would find Unity a wonderful objective,
     and Harmony a remarkable achievement - but the TAO
     does both simultaneously, all the time.

45. Utilise everything that is given, but take nothing.

46. The rich made laws to protect themselves from the poor,
     and now the poor make laws which suppress themselves.
     No wonder there is so much frustration amongst the
     people.

47. It was through conglomeration that we came to be born
     within a human body, and when dispersion takes place
     that will be the final end.

48. Whether right or wrong, be humble enough to say
     "sorry", the incident is then forgotten.

49. Never hinder, never harm and never hurt anyone, either
     by thought or by deed.

50. Think good and do good, and learn to help and serve others whenever you can.

51. No one person owns happiness and understanding, so let the whole world share them.

52. Humanity comprises the whole human race; then let us all learn to work together.

53. You were born, and that is the greatest gift of all, so thank the TAO everyday of your life, for being so generous to you.

54. When death stares you in the face, offer it a hand of friendship, for the TAO has come to meet you.

55. Prayer is the way of the mortals, on this earth, to try and keep in touch with the TAO.

56. If you hurt others, then you will hurt yourself, for this is the repercussion of the TAO.

57.	When the five elements converge to the centre of the Earth, then this world is finished.

58.	Whilst we may be apart, we are not separated, for we are one with the TAO.

59.	A person might steer their car, but it is the TAO that steers the person.

60.	You cannot buy good health or happiness, neither can you buy the TAO, for whilst it costs nothing it is priceless.

61.	If you travel forward when you go to the North, then you must have to travel backwards to go to the South, but as they are both part of the TAO, by standing still, you can travel both directions simultaneously.

62.	Joy and sadness are the expressions of humanity, but the void is the expression of the TAO.

63.	It wasn't by chance that you met your partner, it was arranged by the TAO.

64. There is no such thing as an "accident", it is just a minor Yin incident to let you know that the Yang aspect is to come.

65. When you wash, you cleanse your face and hands. When you have a shower, you cleanse your body. Isn't it time that you cleansed your spirit by bathing in the warmth of the TAO?

66. As a baby we are fully dependent on our Mother as we nestle in her arms, but we must also remember that we are also babies of the universe, so we also depend upon the TAO, which is the Father and Mother of all things.

67. If you recognise ugliness and beauty, then you are a person of the world. If you recognise everything, without comparison, then you are a person of the TAO.

68. Be free of worry, be free of anxiety, be free of fear, be free of lust, be free of ambition, be free of anger, be free of egoism, be free of thoughts. In so doing, you will throw aside these shackles of modern society, and then, and only then, will you be truly free, and an integral part of the TAO.

69. We are completely dependent on the TAO, and must accept its motion, its undulations, its speeds, and its changes, whether we like it or not, and whether it affects us physically, mentally or spiritually.

70. Don't smudge your book of life, for once it is done, it cannot be erased.

71. Be nice to the people that you meet, for it is possible that you will meet them again, one day in a future life, and their spirit has a very long memory.

72. Old age is inevitable, but there is no excuse for senility.

73. If you cannot understand yourself, then how can you possibly expect to understand others?

74. If you detest something, then don't wish it on others.

75. Absolute truth does not fear contradiction.

76. Life and death are inseparable twins, for they affect everyone sometime in their lives.

77. To eradicate the symptom you must first eliminate the cause.

78. If you have complete sincerity, then it can never be torn in two.

79. True meditation is learning to turn the inside out, and the outside in, and the closing of the eyes have nothing to do with it.

80. A little given at a time, can eventually create a mountain.

81. Those who try to escape from the substantial, will not be a part of the insubstantial.

82. People who say they are sorry, admit their mistakes. In this present world they should be sorry all the time.

83. Those who are sick worry about themselves. Those who are healthy worry about everyone else. Those who are one with the TAO have no need to worry.

84. Close your eyes, your ears and your mouth, and in the silence you will see, hear and taste everything.

85. Without emptiness, humanity, our world and the universe, would die.

86. If you have thoughts, then you are harnessing your mind.

87. Ignorance is the foundation of misunderstanding, so open your mind, and you will know all.

88. Those born at the top of the mountain find it difficult to rise any higher, but those born in the gutter can ascend every day.

89. Lies create the bondage of your life.

90. Life is a continuous circle, so don't tarnish your present path, for you could trip up on the muck you have dropped, on the next time round.

91. Our minds and our spirits are free, and so is the whole of nature, then why do we harness our physical lives like we do?

92. Politicians create social sickness, whilst man himself creates his own physical illness - but don't let either of them affect your spiritual growth.

93. When everything in life is fully understood, then words will no longer be necessary.

94. Unless you learn to steer, your boat will keep on drifting.

95. If life means nothing to you, then you are already dead.

96. We are on the bridge of life, so keep moving forward so that you don't hold up the rest of the traffic.

97. Your body is the transport of your spirit, look after it, and make sure it gets regular servicing.

98. The sails of a boat have a very important job to do, but they are useless without the rudder.

99. You will never appreciate perfect happiness until you join the spiritual world, where there are no emotions.

100. You don't have to sit with your eyes closed to meditate, for those who have control of themselves can meditate at any time - even at work.

101. True love will last for eternity.

102. Bad Governments make more and more laws, but good Governments scrap them.

103. If you do good, do not expect thanks. The pleasure of doing is your own reward.

104. Always remember that you could be older than your own Mother and Father, so children of the universe set the example.

105. When you are in trouble, look inward at yourself.

106. Non-involvement means total involvement without emotion.

107. If you want to know your true pathway in life - don't ask a blind man for directions.

108. The ignorant dig for gold, the intelligent tour the world for knowledge, the wise sit still and knows all.

109. When the bad escapes don't look for it, but when the good escapes search yourself.

110. Concentrate on everything that you do daily, it is much better than concentrating an hour each evening.

111. When you have emptied your mind, then you will find it full - and life will take on a different meaning.

112. Don't blame the world for your troubles, for they are self-inflicted, and you have brought them on yourself.

113. The human body harbours five thieves, and if you fail to trap and control them, they will rob you of the essential energy, which is the basis of your life, and you could die.

114. You owe a lot to the TAO of your life, and there is only one way you can repay this enormous debt. Do good and think good all the time.

115. Our fate stops where our destiny begins.

116. If you have the mind, you will have the concentration,
      If you have the will, the job will be undertaken,
      If you have the health, the work will be completed,
      If you have the TAO, you can do anything, anytime.

117. If you mean what you say - then you must have the heart as well as the words.

118. Don't blame the world for your troubles, for they are self inflicted, and you have brought them on yourself.

119. Asking forgiveness on your death bed, is too late, you should have rectified your life whilst you were able to do so, now Yin Kuo (retribution) will take its ordained course.

120. If you can control your mind, twenty four hours a day, then you can control everything.

121. To make progress, help everyone else to advance, and you will be a Teacher of Men.

122. If someone makes a mistake, should we pass judgement? Certainly not! For that was a Yin penalty that the TAO had created.

123. Some touch without feeling,
     Some feel without touching.

     Only a very few can touch or feel without touching or feeling.

124. Those who are fit are not necessarily healthy, those who are good are not necessarily virtuous, both need to change their attitudes to life.

125. In death there is equality for all - then why can't we have this same principle and balance whilst we are all alive?

126. The ignorant have closed everything within themselves, the wise endeavour to understand, the teacher is receptive and keeps an open mind, and the Sage is aware of all.

127. The greater the prize, the greater the ambition and the greater the loss. Don't let your mind blind you to reality.

128. Whether you are leading or following to the rear - the road leads to the same destination.

129. A queue starts with one, a pile starts with one, and even the universe started with one - so remember, rich or poor, you are very important.

130. Those who have no appreciation of life - have no reality.

131. You will always have the answer if you start at the end, and then work your way back to the beginning.

132. If you can eat and sleep contently then your body and mind are at peace.

133. To say sorry after the event is too late, you should have apologised before you started.

134. Your shoe was not made to fit your foot, it was your foot that fits the shoe.

135. Bondage is created by your own thoughts, adopt WU WEI and you will be free for ever.

136. If you cannot trust yourself, then you must mistrust others, but if you believe in the TAO, then trust and mistrust become non-existent, and there is always harmony.

137. If you want to harness yourself - then start thinking.

138. Those who are afraid of death must also be afraid of life.
      If they are afraid of the end, then they must have been
      afraid of the beginning, so living all the years in between
      has had no meaning. What a waste of a life time.

139   You had the audacity to be born, then have the guts to
      live your life, and don't be afraid to die, for there is no
      beginning and no end - for our True Life is perpetual.

140. True freedom starts in the mind.

141. Man is born through parturition, whilst the Sage is born
      through transformation.

142. The causes of hardship and disgrace come from the rich,
      whilst the causes of strife and tension come from the
      poor, and whilst there is still a monetary system there
      will never be equality and neither will there be any
      harmony.

143. What the government considers right for the country, is wrong for the people, but they will never blame themselves for their ego won't allow it.

144. A man of wealth is not necessarily wealthy, and a man of virtue is not necessarily virtuous, for it is only when they have given them away, do they truly obtain the ultimate.

145. Alone there is peace and tranquillity - but complete loneliness is the Void of human emotions.

146. A journey is only as long as the human mind wants to make it.

147. Those who are loved sincerely, will also find that they are hated.

148. Those who give love continuously will one day feel the emptiness.

149. Those who use weapons for war, must expect to die in battle.

150. Those who expect everything and give nothing, will never balance the scales of their life.

151. Why be afraid of death? it does not exist.

152. The more laws that the Governments make, the poorer the poor become.

153. Within strength there is weakness, within weakness there is strength. Men and women are very good examples.

154. Gentleness gives way to force, force gives way to nothing, and is therefore overcome.

155. Those who live like animals, must expect to be like animals, one day.

156. Everything is divisible by one. Yes! The one TAO.

157. Words can lead to war, that is why silence is golden.

158. Spoken words are only the expulsion of air from the mouth, and that air dissipates into the atmosphere and is lost.
The unspoken words are formed and created through good thoughts and good deeds; and as they come from within, they are therefore the truth.

159. When you travel down a new road, you automatically watch out for the signs to guide you. So remember, that every day is a new road in your life, so watch out for the guiding signs - for they are always there.

160. Those who only try to cure the symptoms, are just ensuring that they have a job for life.

161. Watch the Tao at work with the following human activities-

The Dutch in South Africa will eventually be OUT.

The Labour Party in England will slowly fade away to almost nothing.

Christianity is now in its ultimate Yin decline, within two hundred years there will be only a few Cathedrals left to show they ever existed.

Football is also on its final Yin slope, and within a few years, there will only be a few county teams left, for individual clubs will have disappeared.

Just sit back and watch the slow Yin aspect affect the present Russian Empire - the rot has already started.

The Yin aspect has also started for the National Union of Mineworkers in England, and within a few years it will have completely disappeared - as such.

Within a few years women will have the top jobs, and do the majority of outside work - men will stay at home and do the cooking, shopping, and looking after the children, for the Yin slide has started for them, whereas women are now moving into their Yang expansion.

162. If you have no regard for other human beings - then because you are in the same category, you cannot have any regard for yourself, and those close to you.

163. You cannot keep what is not yours - this also applies to a secret.

Chapter 5

Man

Although we developed from the apes twenty million years ago, we should have outgrown the animal instincts within us. Let us work together at all times, to make this a better world to live in, for the sake of our future generations. Let us leave our animal selves behind in the past, and try to develop the full scope and abilities of the future human race.

1.   The greatest treasure that man can own is the TAO, for it costs neither time nor money - and no one can ever take it away.

2.   Discord and conflict are the creations of man - but harmony and tranquillity are the creations of the TAO.

3.   The wise man will always accept the perception and the intuition of his spouse.

4.   Every invention of man can destroy - but he cannot invent anything that can put it all back together again.

5.   A man will truly find himself, if he has an understanding of the TAO.

6.   All men were born free, so stand up and face this reality, for this is the TAO.

7.   No one can hate the man of the TAO, for he who does so, will be encompassed with love.

8. Man coverts wealth. Wealth comes from the earth. Earth was created by the TAO. Then man is a fool and he should get his priorities right.

9. Man cannot mend what the TAO has broken.

10. Man constantly tries to make two from one, if he lived by the one TAO, then he would have the multitude of ten thousand.

11. To gain advantage man will rob his fellow men. Thank goodness there are no advantages within the TAO.

12. The higher a man climbs, the more precarious the journey.

13. Man has three main journeys to make; physically through the Earth's sphere, mentally through the celestial orbit, and spiritually through the heavenly orbit.

14. Man has learnt to utilise that which is useful, but has not yet learnt to use that which is useless.

15. A man at the top of the tree, will feel every breeze.

16. All animals run and jump, but so does man, but who is supposed to do the thinking?

17. It was man who separated men and formed different nations.

18. When man creates an upsurge of violence in the world, watch the counter-part that nature plays - and you will see the work of the TAO.

19. If man can accept a square or a circle, then he must have acknowledged the TAO, which is both.

20. The man of the TAO is not impressed by diamonds, the big houses, or the fine clothes, for he sees them all as just common materials of the universe, created by the TAO, and owned by all.

21. Who is the stronger? The man who runs away: the man who stands and fights: or the man who sits and restrains?

22. Everything that man makes, eventually turns to ruin, but everything that the TAO makes will last forever.

23. The man living in the valley can look all around and upward to the splendour of the mountain, but the man living on the top of the mountain can only look upward, for he would be afraid to look down - so he becomes very isolated and out of touch with the fullness of life.

24. Heaven and Earth are one, it is only man who tries to create a difference.

25. Man tries to embrace immensity with limitations - like an ant trying to embrace an elephant.

26. Man needs words to give advice, the TAO needs no words to give wisdom.

27. Everything in the universe is completely natural, and it is only man that makes it all unnatural.

28. No man can govern others until he has proved that he can govern himself.

29.   Man has lost his natural instincts, and his natural ability, and has therefore lost himself.

30.   Because man has no control over himself, he elects people to sit every day and make new laws, and then he finds ways to break them. Until man learns to understand the laws of the TAO he will have no control over anything.

31.   Man says that we should repay good for evil, but as there is nothing evil and nothing good, then surely repayment is totally unnecessary.

32.   An earthly man loves a number of things some of the time, whereas the man of the TAO loves all things all of the time.

33.   Man has created sickness, pollution, frustration, worry, hate, lust, greed, jealousy, depression, violence, and as they are all YIN, what an ill-balance there is in the world - no wonder there is so little happiness.

34.   If man cannot trust others, then he has lost trust in himself.

35. The man who walks the clouds, has neither his feet on the ground nor his spirit in heaven.

36. When a man cracks the whip, it is other men who feel it.

37. Man plans and creates chaos, but when the TAO plans then everything is perfect.

38. The superior man seems to be alone, but he has a multitude of friends - but those who stand within the midst of the multitude are always alone.

39. Man is taught how to use the right tools for his job, but he must also learn to use the right tools to live in accordance with the laws of the universe.

40. Man in his endeavour to progress invariably steps one pace forward, but in so doing, inevitably takes two paces back.

41. Man detests the sight and smell of dung, yet it gives life and growth to the food that we eat.

42.   A wild horse bucks because it is being harnessed; a man
       bucks yet he is supposed to be free.

43.   Where the feet of a man goes, so the head must follow.

44.   Being conscious is surely being awake, why is it then that
       man is blind every day?

45.   Man studies in his endeavour to learn, but if he lived by
       the TAO, then he would know everything without the
       need for studying.

46.   Modern man has learnt to create illness and sickness, how
       is it that he cannot create the cure?

47.   Man tries to do everything as fast as he can, by not trying
       he would do them all, twice as quick.

48.   The man of the TAO might be dressed in rags, but he has
       untold wealth within him.

49. The greatest treasure that man can own is the TAO, for it costs neither time nor money, and no one can take it away from you.

50. Man loves competitions to prove how good he is, the man of the TAO is already good, so does not have to prove anything to anyone.

51. If man is afraid of death then he must also be scared of living, but the man of the TAO knows that neither exist so there is nothing to worry about anyway.

52. When one man makes a law, then he must expect another man to break it. When there are no laws then there is nothing to break, so both men can live in harmony.

53. Anyone can see the white light, but the superior man, with the help of the TAO, can also project it, so that all men can see it too.

54. Man will leave his footprints in the snow, but the TAO treads the world every second, but leaves no trace.

55. Man knows that he has physical strength. The mind recognises the vitality force within the body, and the spirit automatically accepts macro-cosmic energy; and, whilst they are all separate, they can all be unified by the TAO.

56. On one side, man is connected with nature and the animal kingdom. On the other side, he is connected to the universe. Severe one side and he becomes unbalanced. Severe both sides and he will die.

57. There are three types of man:-
(1) Those who are still a part of the animal world.
(2) Those who grow and develop according to the laws of nature.
(3) The Sage who has made spiritual advancement.

58. Man is severely unbalanced, for his ego and his lust makes him more and more materialistic, and therefore the immaterial, unfortunately, becomes forgotten. So pity man in his scramble for wealth, for the immaterial is the TAO.

59. Whilst man retains his very narrow view of life, then he will see very little. When his vision encompasses the universe, then, and only then, will he see the TAO.

60. It is a long slow climb to the top of the mountain, but
     unless you are extremely careful, it can be a very fast
     return journey.

61. The man of the TAO brings love with him, but those who
     do not believe in the TAO, drive love away.

62. Everything in the TAO is good - and it is only man who
     has upset the balance, by inventing evil.

63. Anyone can throw a stone into a pool of water and cause
     ripples, but the man of the TAO would not throw stones,
     in the first place; and even if he did his stone would not
     cause a splash or any ripples.

64. Man is better remembered for what he did rather than the
     position that he held. The Sage is remembered for what
     he was rather than what he did.

65. Only when man has stopped asking questions will he
     realize that Yes and No have the same meaning.

66.   With complete impartiality all things came into existence, and harmony was perfect. Then along came man who created disharmony through his extremes of love and hate.

67.   Many men act without thinking, so they disregard the feelings of others.

68.   When Arab fights Arab then it is the cracks appearing in the break up of the Arab nation.

69.   When football fan fights football fan, then the sport of football is on its way out. In a few years there will only be a national team left.

70.   When miner fights miner - just sit back and watch the decline of the coal industry. When Yang fights Yang it eventually lands up as a pile of Yin.

71.   The man who talks very little is a pearl of wisdom - but the man that chatters continuously has blown his pearl into thin air.

72. When all men recognise and live by the TAO, and the laws of the universe, then war and racial distrust will disappear, and there will be peace, perfect peace on this Earth. But as man has not been able to attain this state in the last two million years, then it will soon be the turn of the women, and let us all pray that she will make a better job of it.

73. When man has tasted the bitterness within a marriage, can he fully understand and appreciate what true love and true happiness really means.

74. Man will realise one day, that the Yin precedes the Yang, so a misfortune is sometimes an indicator of the Good to come.

75. Man should learn to let everything in life take its natural path, to force it to adopt a line that he thinks is best, is to put it on a rough and dangerous route.

76. Don't try and twist events to suit yourself, otherwise it could be like twisting a strong elastic. Let it go and it will swing back at you.

77. Men who are big mouthed and are constantly talking, might have the words to make them rich, but they are very poor in the heart.

78. Men who start at the beginning have only one objective - the end. But those who try and start in the middle will be lost, for they won't know which way to aim for.

79. Man should always remember that to eliminate the roots of evil, you must pull the top first.

80. If you receive a present open your hand, if you receive advice, then open your mind.

81. Clocks were made by man, but time was made by the TAO, so watch it.

Chapter 6

Woman

The Seahorse, a beautiful yet bizarre sea creature, has the characteristics of many animals. Head like a horse, tail like a monkey, pouches like kangaroos, and roving eyes like a lizard. It is the only mammal known, where the males care for the eggs until they hatch, and then it dies. So the male gives its life for his children. It is also the copyright emblem of the Lee family, who brought the Taoist arts out of China over fifty years ago and the Lee family seahorse only faces to the East.

1.   Man can never take the place of a woman, but women can take the place of a man.

2.   The soft and weak will always overcome the hard and strong, that is why women are superior and live longer.

3.   A man might do the looking, but it is the woman who does the chasing, by standing still.

4.   If you bear a healthy child, then express your thanks to the TAO: but if you bear a sick child, then you have no one to thank, but yourself.

5.   Women usually re-incarnate less times than men, because of their greater spiritual strength.

6.   If a woman is truly healthy she will never have grey or white hair.

7.   If a woman menstruates with the full moon, then her body is working to the natural laws of nature. If she menstruates at any other time in the month, then she is sick, and her body is opposing the natural laws of nature.

8. She is definitely the superior of the two sexes, for he is a greater part of sHE, now although sHE begat he, without she, HE would not exist. So in this world, HE might be in advance of HEr, yet spiritually He is more retarded than sHE, and yet together (HE and HER) they are both here (HE and HER).

9. Yin Kuo is the birth of retribution, don't be the mother of it.

10. She expected everything and yet, gave nothing in return, so she will never balance the scales of her life.

11. Working in the garden one day, she inadvertently stuck a rose thorn in her eye. Now she pays the penalty of her life, through her temporary blindness through the will of the TAO.

12. A woman can describe what is without very easily, but what is within is sometimes beyond description.

13. Women are physically, mentally and spiritually stronger than men, that is why they can support and control the whole family.

14.   Listen to the advice of a woman, for she will FEEL what is right, rather than think what is right.

15.   Women are the kingpins of the whole family health, for she does the shopping and the cooking, and everything depends on these two.

16.   When a woman looks down, she is gaining greater energy and strength, when a man looks down, he's sick.

17.   Women turn Yang as they get older, that is one reason why they natter so much in their later years.

18.   Without women (Yin) the whole world would vanish.

19.   Men have always tried to oppress the females, but in the end, women always come out the winners.

20.   Because women are so Yin, they will never allow anything to go unsolved or unanswered.

Chapter 7

Those I have met

The Taoist Cultural Arts Association was also started through the work started by Chan Kam Lee, and this is also the reason why we have the Lee family crest, which is the Seahorse, as part of our badge. This Association only teaches the Taoist arts which were taught by the Lee family, and they comprise, our Yin and Yang style of T'ai Chi Ch'uan, T'ai Chi Dance, T'ai Chi Silk, T'ai Chi Fan, Stick and Sword. All of which are unique, for nobody else teaches them, and they are all the original Taoist arts, handed down through the Lee family.

1.   Jeanie
     The TAO had put her on the true road of her life, but due
     to her deep state of depression she altered her way
     completely, and now pays the penalty.   Don't let it
     happen to you - learn to flow with the TAO.

2.   She
     She had been on drugs for nine years,
     And her life had become completely empty and lonely,
     She wandered daily, not knowing where to go,
     She had a child whose father she knows not,
     And yet, even that child was born deformed.
     She has now become conscious of the TAO,
     And life has suddenly taken on a different meaning,
     For she is now an integral part of the universe,
     And, at last, there is harmony within and without.

3.   Modern Living
     Her clothes are bought at the best houses,
     She rides in a limousine driven by a chauffeur,
     Yet happiness eludes her.
     Whilst relaxation is in the line of every chair in her home.
     There is no comfort in her heart,
     And sadness is in her eyes and in her actions,
     And her body is tormented by ill health created by her -
     Modern Living.

4.   Depressions
     Her true beauty lay in her mind and in her thoughts.
     Her dedication could not be expressed in words.
     Her interest in life was formulated by her actions,
     And she loved all.
     She gave herself willingly to her parents,
     And to the children of her Sunday School.
     But she drastically altered the WAY of her life,
     Through one simple uncontrollable weakness,
     Her deep depressions.

5. Annie
    She flies when she should walk.
    She runs when she tries to swim.
    She thinks when she should work.
    She practices when she should meditate.
    She travels to one objective along six different routes.
    She goes when she should come,
    And takes a step backward everytime she moves forward.
    She tries to find the Path of her life, and trips over it
     without realizing it.
    The WAY is in front of her all the time, but she keeps
     turning her back to it.
    She has greatness in capacity but smallness in storage.
    She is an integral part of nature, but has lost touch with
     her roots.
    One day she will see the TAO and her self will be truly
    NO self.
    And in losing her self she will have found her True Self,
    For all time.

6. Maureen
    Her eyes reflect the impact of the past, whilst her love is
    held here steadfastly today, and her deep thoughts lead
    her onwards towards the realms of tomorrow. Her body
    contains the damage of the past, while it works
    strenuously for humanity today, and the results of her
    dedication will, no doubt, show up in so many ways
    tomorrow. Her mind vividly remembers everything of
    the past, whilst it strives to conquer the bureaucracy of
    today, so that the unfortunates can gain the benefits of
    her work tomorrow. She has travelled thousands of
    miles in the past, so it is naturally ordained that she
    should remain "still" today, to prepare for the next
    journey tomorrow. Her spirit has laid for her, deep and
    lasting foundations in the past, and it has built for her a
    stalwart building of today, and when her spirit gains its
    roof tomorrow it will be a magnificent house of the TAO,
    for all to see and admire.

7.   Marilyn

She had worked very hard all through her life, and she had borne and brought up a large family of her own. Her part-time work, was working in a children's school, and feeding all the children during the lunch time break. So the TAO had trained her deliberately over the past years, for the most important task of her life. Looking after the interests of thousands, all over the world, for she is now the General Secretary of the International Taoist Society, and she is a mother to them all.

Chapter 8

Just me.

1. Man thinks he is good by flying to Australia in two days, my spiritual guide can do it in one second.

2. I have travelled this way before, but it isn't the same journey.

3. The launderette reminds me of this world, the clothes are tossed around like flotsam, yet in the centre there is nothing but emptiness.

4. I could not read or write at twelve years of age, yet since then I have had the finest teacher ever - the TAO.

5. It is cold and bleak this winter's day, yet within myself I glow with the warmth of the TAO.

6. I am still a child of the universe at 65 years of age, but I know that one day I will learn to grow up.

7. Heaven is not something beyond your reach, for it is all around you even now - join me in recognising it.

8.   Control
      My work takes me all over the country,
      Travelling a thousand miles per week,
      Following the TAO of my life,
      And yet.
      Within myself, I am still endeavouring to seek,
      The complete control of my mind, and my emotions,
      Through the stress and strain of modern living.

9.   My eyes, my mind, and my spirit are always with the
      TAO, whilst my body walks along the ordained pathway
      of my life, on this earth.

10.   I work in the Centre of London, amidst all the hubbub of
      the commercial world, and yet within myself there is
      peace and tranquillity. It is surely the work of the TAO.

11.   I feel within myself that I am never alone, for I know that
      the TAO is always with me.

12.   My mouth must never say "Yes", when my heart says
      "No".

13.   Once I have planted the seeds, then I must have the
      patience to stay around for the harvest.

14.   If I should ever tell a lie, then I know that in the future the truth will have no meaning whatsoever.

15.   I am an orphan, and have been so all my life, yet I know that I have always had a mother and a father, for the TAO has been both to me constantly.

16.   Why should I laugh? there is no happiness; and why should I cry? for there is no sorrow either. For within the TAO there is constant peace and tranquillity without the extremes of human emotions.

17.   You might live a million miles away, yet you can still hold my hand and walk with me along the universal pathway of the TAO.

18.   I shall never be in a position to dig my own grave, for the true Taoist never has a grave - for his dust, after cremation, is given to the land, to help others to survive in the future.

19.   Being deeply in love is a physical yet human emotion - so I am exceedingly happy that I was born, and that the TAO gave me the opportunity of having that wonderful experience in this lifetime.

20. We all make more than a hundred different journeys every day of our life, make sure you learn to understand the Yin and Yang of each one. Just like I had to do, then life will take on a different meaning.

21. When I first started to learn about the Yin and Yang aspect of my own life, and tried to see them at work within my own life, it was then that I remembered these old sayings of my master and teacher. The fire will always fear the water, but the water is never afraid of the fire - as a matter of fact, if it stays long enough, it will enjoy its company and its influence.

22. Human beings try to get to the front of everything, and try to be No.1 all the time. I have learnt, throughout my whole life, that everyone must have a teacher or a leader. Be aware of this, and don't be afraid to take second place, you will get there quicker in the end. A good example is to follow this rule when driving on the motorways.

23. They gather to hear my words, but how can I state that which cannot be spoken? They look to see the WAY, but how can I show it to them when it cannot be seen? They endeavour to lean on me, but how can I supply the crutch they need, for their own support? They expect me to show them the WAY, when their path is always in front of their own eyes. They hope that I can point out the wonders of the Supreme Spirit, yet his work is constantly in front of their eyes. They read of the miracles that have been performed in the past, yet do not perceive those that happen around them every minute of every day. Please Yuhuang Tati, how can I learn to serve them more than I do?

24. I have come to the end of my thoughts at the present time, but as the end is the start of the beginning, you had better watch out for my next commencement, now that I have finished.

Appendix

A Conversation with Marilyn Soo.

Now almost twelve years since Chee Soo died there are many new people training in the Taoist Arts who will never have met him.

Now there's no denying the fact that more than anyone Marilyn was the closest to Chee. So to give you some insight into the character of the man and his writings we have decided to include this transcript of a conversation with her.

If you would like to hear the original recording of this conversation you can find it online in the Biography section about Chee Soo at our Association's website which is located at:

www.seahorsearts.co.uk

A conversation with Marilyn.

...That sounds like a place that Chee and I went to in Australia, it was where the local Australians went for weekends. It was called Rotness Island, and there were no cars on it except for deliveries for the few cafés, there was one hotel on there and it was wonderful. We only went for a day trip and we ended up getting marooned there and had to stay the night. It was on Valentine's day as well. We went over by helicopter, and we were going to come back by the boat but they gave us the wrong times for the boat to leave. Instead of leaving as we thought at half past six it left at half past five, and we all went down to the quay and there was nothing there, and they said:

"Sorry it's gone," hehe, "you'll have to stay the night."

Well the hotel was fully booked.

Oh no, where did you stay?

Well we were eyeing up the upturned boats along the beach and thought "Yes that looks okay" you know, but the friends we were with they bumped into some friends that they knew, and they put us up. So there was the husband, the wife, and three children in this little beach thing, and they put up the four of us, so we were sleeping top to tail and on floors and everywhere, but it was wonderful.

When was that then, when did you go to Australia?

Oh gosh, it must have been about 1988, '87-'88, it was somewhere around there because he went out to Australia to do a course, and we had three weeks out there, two weeks teaching and a week... well, two days in Hong Kong, three days in Singapore, and the rest,...

How did you get to go there then, to Australia?

He had a student out there called Peter, and he invited him over to do a course, so he thought:

"Well why not?"

And we went and it was wonderful, it really was, I really enjoyed it.

Peter and Pat had emigrated out there ten, twelve years, even longer than that, so he just wanted like a refresher course, sort of thing, but he must have told all his students what Chee used to do when Chee was younger, all the tricks, and so that's what they expected him to go out and do, perform all his tricks, and Chee said:

"Well I am not here to become like an animal in the circus, I'm here to teach you, and I'm not going to perform."

And a few of the students were quite upset. And Chee said:

"Well you've come up here, you've come to this course to learn the form and to learn kung fu,"

and not for all the tricks he used to do on chairs and knock people over without even touching them and all that sort of thing that he used to do occasionally.

What was it with chairs?

This is all hearsay from all his older students, that apparently he used to do some fantastic miracle things you know, which were true, but I had never seen them, because they were just one off things that he used to do.

I remember you telling us about when you went on holiday, and they were trying to lift him up.

Oh yes, that was funny, that was in Majorca. We had got to know a couple who ran the café come bar-on-the-beach. Lovely couple, and we used to go in there every day because it was English run - Pepe's it was called - but they were English from Yorkshire. We used to go in every day for a cup of tea, because Chee only drank his own Lapsang tea, and I think it was the second day we went in there and I said:

"Do you mind if - you know - we can only have hot water in the teapot?" I said, "Because he likes to use his own tea."

and they said:

"Yes course he can, whatever he wants," you know.

So he enjoyed his nice cup of Lapsang tea. And then we got talking to them, and over the few years that we used to go out there we got to know them very well, and he helped them out with a few health problems. So when we went over there they put up these posters, and just left them on the bar, and everyone was coming in reading them, and we'd go off and go wandering along the beach, get the deckchairs out, sit there, and somebody would come shake him:

"Are you Chee Soo?" "Ahh, from Pepe's bar, my wife's got a problem with her back" or

"I've got a problem with my arm, and can you...?"

"Oh no we're supposed to be on holiday!" you know, hehe.

Anyway, it got round, and we arranged to take this couple for a meal, and they came to our hotel and we were meeting in the foyer, and somebody said:

"That's that Chee Soo, that these posters are all about."

And this big guy was just like Geoff Capes to look at, and the size of him was absolutely massive, he towered over Chee. And he just went up and he was really challenging Chee you know, and there we were all dressed up in our best ready to go out for a Chinese meal, and he just said:

"Well I've heard that you can pick up people and I bet you can't pick me up."

That sort of challenge.

Chee said:

"Oh well, well you believe what you want to believe." you know.

He said "Well come on then, prove me wrong,"

So Chee looked at me and I says:

"(sigh) Well go on then."

So of course he couldn't pick this feller up, and this feller says:

"Well, oh I can pick you up," that was it, "well you're like a bag of feathers I can pick you up."

and Chee says:

"Well do it twice,"

and he says "Yeah, see, I knew I could pick you up."

and Chee says "Well just do it one more time."

Of course he turns his hands over and he couldn't budge him. And he was going red in the face and he's looking down and he said:

"You've stepped in Superglue or something!" you know, and Chee said:

"No." he says:

"How can I go back home, and say I've met this little tiny Chinese man half my weight, half my size and I couldn't even lift him up off the floor?" he said "I can't go back and tell them that because they wont believe me."

And with that our friends came and we just went out you know. But the funny thing was we had been staying there for a week and they were all German I think in there, and they completely ignored us the whole time, because I think we were the only two British ones in this hotel.   We came down to breakfast next day and they were all saying:

"Hello, hello, hello, you come and sit by me, you come and sit by me."

They just wanted to know him, and sit by him, but it was so funny, this man's face was a picture. He just walked out in disgust and said:

"I can't believe I couldn't pick you up."

I think he must have been some sort of a weightlifter or body-builder, because that's the type he looked you know, and he just couldn't budge Chee at all. But unknown to us we thought it was just him and us two and his mates, but when we looked round we had a whole circle of people watching what was going on you know and I thought -

"Oh gosh this is turning into some sort of comedy show!" you know.

But Chee used to just shrug his shoulders and smile and say:

"Enjoy the rest of your holiday,"

He says, "I can't go home and tell them this!" you know.

We've had some fun times on holidays, because Chee was totally different on holidays, obviously, to when he was teaching. Once he'd finished teaching that was it, he became a different sort of person in a way, there was such a funny side to him, he liked to joke. I mean a lot of people didn't know it but he was a brilliant singer. He had a lovely voice singing, yes, he was a lovely singer,

What sort of singing?

Anything,

Did he do karaoke?

Sort of, yes, he liked modern pop music, funnily enough, really modern stuff you know. Remember when we was at Leamington once, and I think we were doing a Health and Massage course and a bit of yoga, and somebody said:

"It would be nice to do this to Chinese music."?

So previously in the morning I said to Chee:

"We've got some nice Chinese music here we can take one of these tapes tonight."

He says "Okay."

So I played a few and he said:

"Yeah that's nice yes"

He was doing a bit of meditation as well, so he said:

"Yeah we'll take that one."

So I said "Okay" and I left him there and he picked up the machine and got this tape, put it in, it was UB40, haha, oh and everybody just laughed. He just picked up the wrong tape, and it was one of his favourites and it was UB40 of all things.

I remember him saying it was quite good to do T'ai chi to reggae because it was rhythmic music.

Yes

Because they were a Coventry band weren't they?

Yes, at that time they were popular and that's why we'd got the tape, you know, but he liked a lot of modern pop music he wasn't into opera or anything like that, he really liked the modern stuff you know.

What were his favourite bands then?

Well at the time he liked UB40 funnily enough and I don't know why, and the Three Degrees.

Because I heard he used to like The Nolans.

The Nolans he loved, yes, he did.

The Three Degrees?

And the Three Degrees yes, but the Nolans, he loved the Nolans. Oh he used to have it on full blast in his car from here down to

London, it used to drive us mad, especially if we were taking somebody with us. Like if it was Keith or somebody he'd sit in the front and me and Debbie and perhaps Michael would be in the back, it was blaring out and we used to get all the cushions shoved in the loud speakers. Oh if I hear that once more I'll scream, hehe. And then we'd have it all the way back again. Because he was a very fast driver, well he had the name didn't he - "The Flying Seahorse". He put his foot down and he went, but I found out it was a lot of the tapes he was playing, the more faster, the more modern the music it was the more faster he'd go. So I used to say: "Ooh, I've got a new tape here Chee."

It would be slow calm music, and do you know he would slow right down, and then after about half an hour he said:

"Change the tape love."

Hehe.

But if I got a bit panicky and thought he was going too fast I would quickly change the tape and put on a smooth one you know. It worked for a while but he cottoned on to what I was doing I think.

So he used to like singing along to the music in the car?

Not so much in the car but at home you know, he always had the music on when he was working, and when he was writing his books he liked music on.

And he was a dancer too?

Yes

What sort of dancing did he do then?

Well, the jive and the twist. Well he'd do a bit of quickstep and waltz, but if you saw him doing the jive and the twist - we would just sit there gob smacked - and he'd be doing it on his own because I couldn't do it with him, hehe.

I wonder where he learned all that then?

I don't know, the first time I saw him do it was... again this was in Bulgaria, when I went out with my brother and sister-in-law.

We used to go to this same taverna place every night for a meal, and they were fantastic to him, did proper vegetarian meals, as near to Chang Ming as you could get. Because we got to know the girls who used to wait, well they were friends of my brother's, and explained to them that he didn't eat this, he didn't eat that.

"No problem, you just tell us what he'll eat and we'll put it..."

And they used to make him the most fantastic meals, you know. Well when the mealtime was over a group used to come in and play and it turned into like a little tiny dance floor. My brother used to laugh and say... well every now and again his leg would ache especially when you would to go towards the shop and we used to say:

"Yeah he was thinking of the pain in his pocket not the pain in his leg."

When we were going shopping. Well we'd go back to this place, have a meal, and as soon as the music came on he would say:

"Come on, lets get up and dance!"

And he would be the first one up there dancing, and he'd start the jiving and the twisting and I'd think:

"I don't believe this!" you know.

Then he'd sit down, but it got so that the music wouldn't start until Chee walked in. So if we went a bit later the band wouldn't be playing. They used to say:

"Ahh, here comes our old man, now we can start." you know.

And the music would go on and he would get up and dance and everybody else would get up and dance, so they got to that they wouldn't start the music until Chee walked in.

That was in Bulgaria?

That was when we went to Bulgaria yes.

Did you go a few times?

Yes, we went a few times out there yes, he liked it out there it was...

He liked the people didn't he? He said to me.

Oh he loved them yes, absolutely loved them.

He said they were very nice pleasant, simple...

You know they were so poor you wouldn't believe how poor, and the wages they got. I mean I'm talking a few years ago, well not that long ago.

Ten or twelve years, well fifteen years?

But my brother had been going out there for about fifteen years or more, and he got to know the one family very well, they become close friends and then they just said:

"We'll fetch my sister and her husband out, next time we come."

"Fine."

We goes out there, and the father and the mother of the friends they met invited us to their place one evening for a meal. It was way up into the hills into the back of beyond, and they were telling us how much money they get for working a week or for a month. Top dentists were getting the equivalent to £15 a month out there, they were so poor, but the feast they put on was unbelievable. And everything is natural out there, there's no such thing as chemicals and additives in the foods and preservatives. Everything was off the land, and that's how they used to live out there, but the food was second to none, it really was.

What was the name of the place in Bulgaria?

Golden Sands. But this was up in... where we went I don't know the name of the place you know, way up into the mountains where they lived. And I mean they were so poor it's unbelievable, you can't believe how they can survive. And you used to see the women on the dust carts and on the water carts in the height of the tourist season emptying the dustbins you know, driving the big bin lorries. And you used to say:

"Well where's all the men?"

"Well they're out working the land."

They were out working the land so the women had to do the things in the tourist areas in the hotels and the bins and the big water lorries that used to go round. And God they used to work so hard.

It must be quite a natural environment, not as many factories and stuff.

No, I can't even think now what they produce in Bulgaria, as such, you know I can't think of anything.

You don't really see 'Made in Bulgaria' very much.

No you don't. And most of it is farmland and in winter they've got the skiing. You know they've got the very, very cold winters, and then they've got the very hot summers. I honestly cant think of anything that they produce to survive. So whether they just survive on tourism I don't know.

I suppose Chee came from quite a poor background really didn't he, so he'd get along with people like that?

Well, with Chee he always had a slight chip on his shoulder because he had had some bad experiences when he was living in London, about being with a Chinese face you know. And I had seen it with my own eyes when we were in Coventry. He'd be the last one to be served even if he was first one in the queue, well I saw that with my own eyes. Silly little remarks that people would say as we would walk by like "Slanty eyes" or "Chinky". So he always had this little bit of a chip on his shoulder. So when anybody was nice to him he was absolutely shocked. Especially when we went to Wales, he couldn't believe it. And he absolutely loved it down there, because we were walking along a lane to go to the next town one day, it was a lovely day and I said:
    "Well let's walk into town to save getting the car out."
    And we met this chap coming the opposite way with a dog, and as we crossed this man says:
    "Good morning, how are you? Lovely day isn't it?'
    And Chee just smiled and he said:
    "That man doesn't know me and he said hello!"
    And I says:
    "Well yeah, well why shouldn't he?"
    and he says:
    "Yeah but me with my face!"
    And that's when it hit me thinking - "He must have had some rough times", you know, that he'd never sort of spoken about.

So people were quite racist?

Yes, and then we went into the next village, in Brynmawr. And going in the shops there, and everybody spoke to him - and then over the years he was down there - and saying:

"Well what are you going to buy here today?" or "What are you going to do today? Why don't you sit down and let her wander around?" and "Do you want a cup of tea?"

And they'd make such a fuss of him - and not because he was Chinese and they'd never seen a Chinese before - because there's Chinese takeaways down there and whatever. But they just seemed to take to him, and it just took his breath away sometimes. He couldn't believe how many people would help him if like the car broke down or whatever.

I think when he was young in London - at that time there weren't that many Chinese in Britain at all.

Yes, and I think he had a bit of a rough time. I don't mean he was assaulted or beaten up or anything like that, but I think he was very much a loner, it made him a loner, because he was an orphan

when he met Chan Lee. It must have been great, that shows how weird that must have been

to see another Chinese face. Just by playing football in the park and it hit this man and this man turned round and he had a face like Chee's - like a Chinese - and that's how they got talking and one thing and another and got to know each other.

Because he didn't have his father, his own father, did he?

Yes, he obviously doesn't know much about him, because he was just a baby. I don't know how old he was when his father died but he couldn't have been more than a year or two old. And then his mother died when he was four or five so he didn't know his parents as such. The only thing he could remember was somebody taking him to what he believes was a hospital type of place, and he saw this woman lying in bed and he didn't know who she was or why he was taken there. It was only afterwards when he grew up and his memory - he started remembering things - and he thought:

"They must have been taking me to see my mother when she was dying."

So he doesn't remember anything about his mother or his father.

That's very sad isn't it?

It is, and because there were no other Chinese people around as well he must have felt so lonely and so alone. Even though he had good foster parents or whatever, it's still different when you're a child growing up and going out or going to school. That there wasn't anybody else that even looked like you, you know? So whether he was picked on, or made fun of I don't know.

Well it's funny because I was just talking to a man on Saturday who's also Chinese and he said "Oh well I was bullied a lot, sometimes people would respect me but if anybody wanted to be horrible then they would pick on me."

No doubt that's what happened to Chee, I don't know because he... of all him being a great master, he himself was a very insecure man, very insecure. Every time I went out of the house he was waiting, watching every bus coming to the bus-stop to see if I was on it, and every time if I went out, if I went to go into town for a bit of shopping and he was busy in the house, I would go into town on my own and back, and when I got off the bus, and the bus-stop was almost opposite where we lived, a walk across the road, he would have a cup of tea in his hand waiting for me.
" I didn't think you was going to come back"
"Why?!"
"I don't know, I just got this feeling that you know you'd left, you weren't coming back."
I said:
"Well I wouldn't go without my clothes"
I used to make a joke out of it:
"Oh, I wouldn't go without my clothes, and I wouldn't go without this, and I wouldn't go without that."
And then he'd just smile you know:
"Well it did cross my mind, because I don't know what you're doing with me, you know?"

And then we went to America - and Dave from Wales will tell you the same - Chris and I went in to see a show, and it was a boiling hot day, so Dave and Chee sat outside looking at whatever was going on not far from this big tent that Chris and I went into. We went to see like a sort of a show with horses and something, and they weren't really interested so they stayed outside. And then Dave told me after, every five minutes he kept saying to Dave:

"Do you think they're alright?"

Dave said: "Yeah they're alright, they're sitting in there watching a show."

"Ahh, right, okay."

Five minutes would go by:

"Do you think we had better go and look for them?"

"No, they're fine, lets go for a walk."

"We'd better not go far because they might not know where we are."

"Well, they'll stay here."

"Oh. Alright. No, I think we had better go in and find them."

And he said in the end he drove him mad, we were only in there three quarters of an hour, but he said if he asked once he asked a dozen times.

"Should we go in, make sure they're alright?"

He was so insecure in a way.

He was a very humble man though wasn't he?

Oh, he was so humble, oh he was, I mean when he met the coloured boxer, Frank Bruno, down in Bristol. Frank Bruno had heard about him and he'd read his book apparently. And so they said:

"He's coming down this weekend."

and he (Frank Bruno) said:

"Well I'd like to meet this guy."

So they arranged for us to meet him. And I said to Chee:

"Oh, Frank Bruno..."

"What's he want to see me for? Because he's the big man, I'm not, I'm a nobody, why does he want to see me?"

I said:

"Well he's heard about you, he's read your book and he'd just like to meet."

"But I'm a nobody, I'm a nothing, and he is the big man" you know.

And he couldn't understand why he wanted to meet him, as I said he was very, very humble.

And at that time he was having a hundred people in the hall! So how come he didn't think he was...?
Because he never thought of it like that?

No.

That's the way isn't it? That's why he was such a good master.

I mean obviously he was, teaching Kung Fu and the fighting Arts or the weapons or anything like that nobody could beat him, but in the house he was the most gentle kindest person you could ever wish to meet you really could. You know he had a heart of gold, he would do anything.

Did he get very tired?

He did get tired yes, but there again...

How did he deal with that though?

When you think I met him when he was sixty two so he wasn't a young person. When you think at sixty two going on seventy two you would get tired wouldn't you? Especially doing martial arts and trying to write and then travelling all over the country you would begin to get tired, you would begin to slow down. Because he never stopped. Alright he worked weekends doing the courses, but he never stopped in the house - from the minute he got up and had his breakfast he was at his typewriter all the time and in books all the time checking up on this and comparing notes with one thing and another, he just never stopped.

Still learning wasn't he, always, as well?

Yes, because a lot of his work had gone up in flames in a house he lived in years ago when he was a salesman and he was out, and he came back, and he was renting a thatched cottage and it went up in flames. And all his work went with it, all his notes like from Chan Lee and everything they just -
phhhh! So, gradually he tried to remember things, you know, and you can't remember everything. And sometimes you write things down like some Art or some form, then he'd go through it and think: "That's not working out right, that's not right, that doesn't flow right, that doesn't..." you know, he never stopped.

All the health stuff as well , all the massage notes and all that, that's a lot of work as well isn't it?

Yes, which meant he had a lot more research to do, an awful lot.

And then he had a lot of his notes stolen from Alderman Callow School. I mean why he ever took his briefcase I don't know. He would prepare on the Friday night and he'd say to me:
"What are we doing this weekend?' and I'll say:
"Oh it's Health and Massage this weekend."   you know, or whatever, or:
"It's the students T'ai chi and Kung Fu." or "Its the Instructors' T'ai chi" or whatever.
So he would get all his notes, prepare them, or put them in his briefcase, put them on the bench and never opened them. Very rarely did he go into his briefcase:
"Oh yes, what did I plan today? Oh well, never mind."
And so he'd fetch home the briefcase the same way he took it down, unopened. But one day he got his notes out for somebody to check on something, left them there, and they were gone!
It could have been an accident, a mistake, but if somebody had gone home with his notes they would have known, or fetched them back or rang him up and said:
"I've picked these up by mistake" wouldn't they? I would have thought.

So he used to help people out quite a bit didn't he? Behind the scenes?

Oh yes, and there were always people coming to the house.

What, with health problems?

Yes, and he'd go out as well to people, I mean he never charged a penny you know, and they would ring him up all hours of the day and night and say:
"Can you come down?'
Whatever it was, in Coventry or Birmingham, and he'd go out and try to help them and it was all free, he wouldn't charge anybody anything, you know? All he would do would be to give them the Chang Ming diet and then different herbs or different poultices or whatever, I mean he didn't administer anything because - well he wouldn't - but he used to sit them down, talk to them.

He might give them a massage, but you know he wouldn't charge
a penny, he just wouldn't, that just wasn't him. Because his
opinion was:

"I got it for nothing so I'll give it for nothing!".

I mean he had to charge for the hall obviously because he had
to pay for the hall.

Yes, and that caused a problem one day when the Lord Mayor
turned up didn't it? Do you remember that: when the Lord Mayor
turned up? It was on a Saturday morning and we were all in there
- I think it was an Instructors course - and we were all in there
training, and then one of the staff at Alderman Callow came and
said:

"Marilyn can you ask Chee to move his car?"

"Why?"

"Because we're expecting the Lord Mayor any moment and
he's coming to have a look round the school." Because it was one
of the newest buildings built you know? And they wanted to
come and:

"So will you ask him to move his car?"

So I says:

"You are joking!" I said:

"There's no way on God's earth will I go and ask him to move
his car! If you want to ask him to move his car you go in and ask
him," I says, "but I'm not!"

So he says: "Why?"

And I says:

"Just take it from me, I wouldn't even bother if I were you!"

Because his car was his pride and joy wasn't it? And we had
parked there for years and years and years, in the same place, not
blocking anybody in, it was like a little sort of cul-de-sac wasn't it?
So you couldn't go anywhere once you had parked there. And I
said:

"Well why does the Lord Mayor's car want to go in his place?"

"Well it won't be so far for the Lord Mayor to walk will it?"

Because if you remember rightly you went up the driveway but
you had to back out, and there was just enough room to drive up.
And I said:

"Well I 'm not asking him, I value my life more than that."

"Well he's got to move it."

"You go and ask him."

So he says: "Okay"

So this chap went in, he was the Headmaster or whatever, and he said:

"Oh Mr Soo do you mind moving your car?"

He says:

"Why, what's the problem?"

You know, he thought there was a problem.

He said:

"Oh it's just that the Lord Mayor is coming to visit us."

and Chee said:

"So?"

He says: "Well would you mind moving it down to the bottom to the car park?"

He says: "Excuse me, I'm paying for this today, and I've been paying for it for years and years and years, I've put a lot more money into the school than what the Lord Mayor has!" hehe.

And he went: "Oh, so you're not going to move your car?"

and he said: "No, I'm not going to move my car, unless you don't want me to teach here any more." he said, "Then I'll pack up the class here and now and we wont come back here ever again!"

And he says: "Oh no, no, no, don't take that attitude Mr Soo."

He says: "Well put it this way, who comes here more often me or the Lord Mayor?"

And he says: "Well yes but he is the Lord Mayor!"

He says "I don't care who he is!"

So, and I was laughing, and I thought I would rather you argue with him than me,

Then after a bit he calmed down, and this fellow went off and he said to Des:

"Des, get my keys, and move my car."

By the time Des came out the Lord Mayor had come up and his driver had to park behind Chee then, and the Lord Mayor had got out and he walked round. It wasn't the Lord Mayor's fault, he didn't care two monkeys where he parked you know, it was a lovely sunny day and he said it didn't make any difference. So I went out and had a word with the driver, and I was laughing with him, I said:

"Sorry about this but" I said "well my husband wouldn't move his car."

He said: "I don't blame him, I wouldn't move my car either, because he's only going to be here five minutes and then he's going." and his own chauffeur just laughed as well. But it was just the attitude of the Headmaster of the school. That was so funny, and Des was hopping from one foot to another going:

"What do I do, what do I do?"

I said:

"Just leave it, it'll sort itself out."

How did Des start training, do you know?

Before my time, he knew him from quite a few years before, the same as Tony, the two Tonys: Tony Swanson and Tony Ellison. Because I think Tony Swanson was the last one I met out of the three of them.

There were so many rumours going around that Chee was dead, that he had emigrated to Australia or New Zealand, and then he had emigrated to France, and he was living there. There were so many rumours floating around, it was as if Chee had disappeared off the face of the Earth. For about four or five years nobody knew where he was and what he was doing. He was still down in the London area and then he moved up to Coventry, and then we sort of got things kick started again and then contacted a few people, well obviously by this time people had moved away. And gradually it filtered through to different people and they came back. And then I remember Tony walking in and I didn't know who the hell he was, and I didn't realise he was one of the old guys from before, you know, and Tony Ellison as well, and Des. They were the three main ones around at the time.

So how did you first get to meet Chee?

It was at my son-in-law's house. He was with my daughter, they weren't married then, and it was her twenty-first birthday, and this was in Coventry, at the beginning of February, a bitter cold, freezing day, and the motorways were closed because they had had a lot of snow. Chee was in the process of moving up here so he was storing a lot of his stuff in Keith's house, and this Saturday they had told everybody not to go on the motorway, 'if you do you go at your own risk', because it was so bad. Of course well Chee took no notice of that and he just shot up the motorway, and apparently after he had gone through they closed the road off anyway, just for safety reasons, because they had had a lot of snow

And he turned up at Debbie's house - at Keith's house - not knowing that there was a birthday party going on, and that's where I met him.

And the reason I went over there was that my son who had been living in Nigeria at the time had come over and he wanted to see Debbie and Keith, you know his sister, and where she was living. So I says:
"Well I know where it is but you'll have to take me over."
So we went over there and we were having a bit of a party.

So Keith's your son-in-law?

Yes, and he used to be one of Chee's students, so he knew Chee very well, he had been training with him for years and years and years, and then he said to Keith one day:
"I'd like to live in the Midlands, I'd like to move up, will you send me down information on houses from the estate agents?"
So Keith used to collect all the stuff from the estate agents, either send it to him or wait for him to come up and give it to him and he'd look through:
"Oh that's got no garage, and that's no good, this one looks okay, and that's out of my price range."
Or whatever you know, he'd filter through them until he had a little pile of those that might be okay. But in the meantime he started moving a lot of his paperwork up and a lot of his personal stuff up to keep in Keith's house. And then we turned up, and then halfway through the party - it was a sort of late afternoon party not a night party - there was a knock on the door and it was Chee turned up with some more of his stuff, and very embarrassed that he didn't know that it was anybody's birthday. Shook hands with me and he said:
"You've got varicose veins."
Now it was in the middle of winter and I had trousers, I had boots on, I had coats, and I had everything. And he said:
"Your circulation's very bad," and he said "I bet you've got varicose veins."
And he was absolutely right, hehe.

That's a nice way to greet you!

I thought: "Oh, strange man!" hehe.

And they wanted him to stay the night, but because there was a party on he felt quite embarrassed so he said:

"No, no, no I'll go."

And he travelled all the way back, he stayed for half an hour or so and then he travelled all the way back down to London. The weather was absolutely atrocious, it was terrible. He just came up on a whim, he thought: "I've got nothing on this afternoon I'll just nip up there" but the weather was so bad. But secretly I found out afterwards because he'd got his new car that week and he wanted to try out his new car, he wanted to give it a run on the motorway.

Was it white?

Oh yes of course, always white, he only had one other one and that was blue, and he kept that for three months I think, then he changed it so, every car since then had to be.

So when he came up here he didn't work anyway?

No, he had retired years ago. But no, he had to have a white car, and it had to be a Vauxhall car as well, but then he took a fancy to these little Jeep type things, and he thought:

"I quite fancy one of them."

Because he sat in one and he was quite high up, and he thought:

"Well that's good I can see everything."

You know, and anyway we had it for about three months and I know he was going down to see Tony Chan in Hatfield, just to visit him, and he was driving along and he said:

"This car won't do no more than seventy!" and he said: "Look there's a flippin' man on a push-bike overtaking me now!" hehe.

So he kept it about three months then took it back to the garage and he said:

"No, can't cope with this!"

So he got rid of it and then he got a normal car. But it made me laugh he said:

"It comes to something when somebody on a push-bike can overtake me!"

Well it wasn't, it was just his way of putting it you know, because he used to like to put his foot down. He changed his car nearly every year didn't he? because the joke was as soon as the ashtray was full he changed his car, hehe.

You know Chan Lee was his teacher, did he have any other teachers?

No, he met other teachers, but never actually, as far as I know, had any other teachers.

He trained with them?

Well when you say trained with them he might have gone for a weekend course with them, because they were like that:
"We'll come to your course you come to our course."
Or there was one particular café in London that he used to go to, and I think a lot of the Chinese orientals used to go into this café and they used to get talking, and one said:
"Oh I run this sort of club."
And Chee said:
"Well I do kung fu."
And somebody did Karate and:
"Oh why don't you come along to one of ours?"
And Chee said:
"Yes okay."
And then he'd say:
"Well why don't you come to one of mine?"
But that doesn't mean to say they taught each other, they just went to see how the other clubs worked, and what the other Arts were you know, but he had great fun with the... I think it was the Karate club he went to, somebody invited him to. They lined all their men up, and said:
"Well see if you can get through without them touching you."
And he did, he went from top to bottom and not one of them could touch him.

Aikido?

Aikido was it? I couldn't remember.
And he says:
"Right I'll make you..." whatever belt they have in that Art I don't know, and Chee says:
"I'm not interested, I just want to stick to my own." you know.

I remember him limping sometime towards the end, but then I suppose reading that piece of paper that you gave me last time I came round, about the way he was treated in the prisoner of war camp.

I don't think it was that, well, you know what he died of, an abdominal aneurism, and I think – it wasn't so well known when he died - but I think it was probably thrombosis, a blood clot that moved up his leg.

Because he had been on quite a long plane journey?

We had done an awful lot of flying the previous two years, I mean long distance like to America, Kenya, and Australia you know, and then the European countries, we seemed to have done an awful lot of flying. Well thrombosis wasn't linked to flying at that time, it was only after that they said that long haul flights can cause thrombosis. Because he had been limping off and on for about three years, before he actually died.

It's going to catch up with you isn't it?

And we noticed it and he used to say:
"It's cramp."
Because he said:
"I'm not going to the doctor's with that leg."
You know, never even thinking of thrombosis. Well I just said:
"There's something wrong with your leg because you keep rubbing it."
And he said:
"Oh it's only cramp, it'll go."
And he used to rub it and massage it, and it did go. And then it turned into a joke, because every time we went out - especially with my brother and his wife, or on holiday - as soon as we got to the shops this pain would come, and we'd say:
"Yeah you're thinking about the pain in your pocket aren't you? The pain in your leg goes up to your pocket."
Because we'd come to dress shops or whatever sorts of shops or markets. Having said that he used to love shopping anyway, and it just turned into a joke you know, because we used to say:
"How come he doesn't get a pain in the leg when he's up dancing?"

And you know it was that sort of banter we used to have with him, but he used to go out say once a week whenever the dustbin men came, and he'd collect everybody's dustbins in and take them to their gardens, big heavy things you know?

And I said:

"Well why are you doing that?"

And he said:

"They're all in work" you know "and they would have to do it when they come home".

And they were neighbours that we didn't really talk to much? Next door, Patrick opposite, and then somebody else two doors down, he would fetch our own bin and and then he'd go round taking everybody else's bins in. And he'd come back with his leg hurting, and I said:

"You shouldn't have done that."

And then he'd walk perhaps down to the post office, fine, but walking up his leg would hurt, and it got more and more regular, but you hardly ever saw it on the training days. I could tell when it was starting, but nobody else knew.

Because he had Malaria as well didn't he?

Oh he had Malaria yes, but this was something that's probably caused through smoking perhaps, and a lot of flying.

I remember he had scars on his legs...

Oh he had scars up his legs, yes.

On that piece of paper it says about him being staked out in the sun for seven days, and nearly going blind, and then when he came back he was four stone, he had lost his teeth, his hair.

Well they used to put them on double rations - as they called it - when they came back from being prisoners of war, they used to give them double rations of food, and they put him on treble rations because he had lost that much weight, so he was allowed three times as much as anybody else.

That's going to be quite a strain on your system, it's going to age you isn't it?

Oh gosh yes, and then when he escaped they were only allowed a little bit of rice here and there and everywhere, and he escaped with a Gurkha and the Gurkha was from that region, and he knew what herbs were good or what was bad. So they used to eat a lot of herbs as well, and he says that's what got us through to the other side - him and this Gurkha chap - because he had a great knowledge of the local herbs, and what fruit or berries you could eat. Because some of them obviously were probably deadly poison, but this Gurkha knew exactly which ones you could eat, what leaves you could eat and what you couldn't eat. So they escaped over the mountain until they got to somebody who took them in and looked after them.

He had quite a long time with Chan Lee really didn't he, in a way? He met him when he was about twelve or something, and he had that time before the army?

Yes, but he didn't have that much time after did he, when he came back, because then Chan Lee died didn't he?

He died in 1954 didn't he?

I mean he was a traveller was Chan Lee, back and forth to China on the boat, and then the boat capsized and he died, so he didn't have an awful lot of time with him after because he was only over here for a few weeks or whatever before he would have to get back on his boat to go back again.

So yes, he had quite a hard upbringing you know, he had some nice foster parents but he had some that weren't so nice, but on the whole I think he had fairly good foster parents, they used to farm them out in different places, but in those days, unlike today - if there was a family they would try to house all the family together wouldn't they under one foster care - but one sister went to one foster home his other sister went to another foster home, and they lost touch. So he really did feel alone, as such, you know? And one of his foster homes was up here in Warwickshire.

In Leamington?

In Leamington wasn't it? yes.

Barnardo's?

It was in a Doctor Barnardo's home and from there they fostered him out into a house somewhere in Warwickshire, and I can't remember exactly where it was.

The Taoist Cultural Arts Association

You may be interested to know that this Association is based on the foundations that were originally laid down by Professor Chan Kam Lee, who started the first Chinese Taoist Arts School in London in 1930.

Chan Lee died in the winter of 1953-4, when his boat sank in a fierce storm off the coast of China, and it was then that his nephew Chee Soo was asked to take over the Presidency of all the Taoist Arts that were being taught. In 1958, Chee Soo set up coaching classes with the object of training qualified teachers, county, area and regional coaches. Over the years these have proved very successful and there are now classes and clubs operating in many parts of the world, besides those that exist in the British Isles. Our Association teaches the Taoist Health Arts, Taoist Cultural Arts and also the Taoist Self Defence Arts.

Taoist Health Arts

'The Eight Strands of the Brocade', which comprise:

Ch'ang Ming	—Taoist Long Life Dietary Therapy
Ts'ao Yao	—Taoist Herbal Therapy
Wen Chiech'u	—Contact Thermogenesis
An Mo	—Taoist Massage
Hsia Chen Pien	—Acupuncture
Tien Chen	—Taoist Spot Pressing (Acupressure)
Ti Yu	—Physical Culture
Chili Nung	—Ch'i, Li, Vibration and Palm Healing

Taoist Cultural Arts

Tai Chi Ch'uan	—The Supreme Ultimate
K'ai Men	—Taoist Yoga (Chi Kung)
I Fu Shou	—Sticky or Adhering Hands
Li Kung	—Taoist development of Li energy
Mo Kun	—Taoist Wand — external energy control
Mo Hsiang	—Taoist Meditation

Also Tai Chi Sword, T'ai Chi Silk, Tai Chi Stick and T'ai Chi Dance.

Taoist Self defence Arts.

Feng Shou	—'Hand of the Wind' Kung fu, soft and

gentle but very fast, and suitable for all age groups.

Chi Shu	—Taoist form of Aikido

and all the other forms of the Taoist fighting arts including such weapons as sticks, flails, swords and chopsticks.

Needless to say, all three sections of the Taoist Arts work together, and all strictly maintain the traditions that were laid down by Chan Kam Lee and his family.

Our teacher Chee Soo, was naturally also a Taoist, and his whole life was dedicated to serving the sick and suffering, and to helping humanity whenever possible.

Anyone who is interested in any of these arts can attend the student classes which are held regularly in the British Isles and on the Continent. Weekend courses are also held, together with courses at Easter and Christmas and in the Summer. For more details please contact:

The Taoist Cultural Arts Association
Our website is located at:

www.seahorsearts.co.uk

Other titles in the series

Taoist Arts of the Lee style
by Chee Soo

The Chinese Art of T'ai Chi Ch'uan
The Taoist Way to mental and physical Health.
A dynamic aid to health and inner tranquillity through
controlled movements for self-defence and the development of
physical and mental powers.

The Taoist Art of K'ai Men
Opening the door to your inner self through Chi Gung
Physical rejuvenation and mental vigour through this ancient
and powerful system of energy utilization.

The Tao of Long Life
The Chinese Art of Ch'ang Ming
Health and long life using a time tested approach to diet and
nutrition that has been practised by Taoists for thousands of
years.

The Taoist Ways of Healing
The Chinese Art of Pa Chin Hsien
An introduction to the complete system of ancient Chinese
Taoist health arts the 'Eight Strands of the Brocade'.

The Taoist Art of Feng Shou
'Hand of the Wind' Kung Fu
A complete illustrated guide to this unique system of self-
defence which combines 'softness' with speed to great effect.

Published by Seahorse Books
For more information visit our website at:
www.SeahorseArts.co.uk
or Email us at
SeahorseBooks@seahorsearts.co.uk